WHAT MY HAIR SAYS ABOUT YOU

Published by Metatron
www.onmetatron.com
305-5555 Ave. de Gaspé, Montreal QC H2T 2A3

Editing | Ashley Opheim
Layout and book design | Ashley Opheim
Cover design | Eric Amling and Laura Theobald

First edition
First printing

We acknowledge the support of the Canada Council for the Arts, which last year
invested $153 million to bring the arts to Canadians throughout the country.

Canada Council   Conseil des arts
for the Arts   du Canada

WHAT MY HAIR SAYS ABOUT YOU

LAURA THEOBALD

Metatron
Montreal

what my hair says about you

when a field of you
is ripe in me
i am dead to you
sometimes i'm just
walking
& i fall
i don't even wear tall shoes
inexplicable hair ·   · * . *
i gave up something for you
& i'm not sure
what it was

hello i'm bad

i need a man for every mood
i'd like to dream in death
i like you
& i like to defy your sweetness
with the pomp of a big
fat
secret
can i give you this
laurel wreath
wove together by
another man
i want to do evil things
while i'm inside you
i only believe in this one
pit hardening
in my stomach

& the face
that i am sucking on
that it is not your face
hello i'm bad

mindpower

today you are mean to me
& i'm only happy when
i'm tossing you
into a dumpster
right now i'm tossing you into a dumpster
with the power of my mind
next i'm forgiving you
like a cat
forgiving another cat
now i have cats in my poems
& it's all over
now i'm tossing you into a dumpster

zen

i'm writing in synthetic light
what it feels like
is days
coming between us
i mean i haven't seen the sun
in days
& i'm sleeping
like i'm already dead
which seems like too literal a way
to have interpreted the koan
saved to my desktop
i both think i'm going to die
& don't
give
a fuck
which doesn't feel at all
the way you'd think of as zen

you tell me i sound weird

you tell me i sound 'weird'
& that 'maybe' i should
'talk to someone'
i try to imagine which
of the latest series of
traumatic events has
affected my speech patterns
you say i'm being dramatic
& i complain too much
& idk what 'real poverty' is
i say i'm clinically depressed
& that there's only
one thing keeping me alive
but i can't remember what
we can't figure
who's right & who

should be loved more
sometimes i'm aware you're
more upset than me
you say you literally
just punched your phone
i think it's funny
sometimes i can't tell who's
more upset
sometimes it's me

the south

i go to a thing
where nobody knows me
then to another thing
where nobody knows me
cool
i'm late for this thing
look at the girl walking in late
even the one singing
into the microphone
turns to look
cool
she is singing a white stripes song
i know this song
i'm typing
while walking at night
it will appear to others that i'm

unaware of my surroundings
but look
there's a cat
look
there's a rope
caught in the armpit of a tree
look
the south at night
it stinks like an all-night restaurant
in the morning
there's water everywhere
but you can't swim in any of it

a kind of place

i feel like i'm entering
a kind of place
where
no one answers a text
at 3 in the morning
or at least
nobody i want to
have sex with
there's only one person
i want to have sex with
but that person
i don't think exists
so
what i'm saying is
is anybody awake
in the year 2000

& are you wearing
the skin of someone
or any skin
& also
how did i get so
dying
&
but
since
nobody is awake
in that year
or any year
i guess i haven't
grown up yet
i'm entering
a kind of place
& it is stupid

let's be

let's be in a funk together
let's be in a river together
called the mississippi
let's be in on
one thing
together
& let's let that one thing
be
the grieving
let's grieve until
we've grieved all the things
& later
when we've grieved
those things
let's grieve
the other things
we didn't know about yet

dumpster

will someone please
throw me into that dumpster
i'm finally ready
to be still
& moth-eaten
remember when we were
brave like
money &
what
i could know how to smile then
i stuffed my mouth with a sock
i carried you till saturday
& i could still do that
but i forgot how to smile

i am magic

i am a magician
i make you love me
& i make you hate me
at the same time
i say love in a poem
& i am the poet rumi
when i breathe the air
i don't have to think
when i kiss you i am
kissing you
& that is a good time
not to think
when i am thinking
i am not alive
& not dead
i make a third thing

i call upon the oracle
& i am the oracle
& i am the stones
& your eyes are stones
& i look into the stones
& see your eyes
& it makes me sad
& i cry sparkle drop tears
till they collect in a puddle
in my throat
& i don't move
until the puddle
evaporates

holy man

today i think
kissing you
would be like
kissing
a holy man
& i think
you are
a holy man

i fell in love with a bad man

my mother sold me demons
that is why my hands crawl
at night
his hooves are kicking me
in his sleep
he is like a moonbeam
when he talks
in his sleep
when i am in love he says
she was a good woman
yes & i am a bad man

confused what kind of animal i am

there's a very real sense
in which someone
has lost everything
do you feel bad
i do
but i don't feel bad for you
i keep throwing you bones
& you keep saying
throw me
a goddamn bone
like
these are my bones
motherfucker
even a snake has bones
what am i
a jellyfish
i don't live in a watery tomb

except on tuesday
on tuesday
i live in a watery tomb
& i have bones
a whole pile of them
to sit on
& worry over
like a gollum
but today i'm a cat
& i'm not really
hearing all this
desperate
everything
i can't
really find
a name for
i need a dictionary for feelings

that's how far out it's gone
so far out
i'm a flamingo
which is a kind of joke
the lawn ornament
of the animal world
unless i'm misinterpreting
its pinkness
which i think
has something to do with
you are what you eat
or
what is the animal for
having made
the most egregious error
that must be
a whale or
a dinosaur

when i'm a forest

when i'm quiet in our love
i'm a quiet forest
i'm a forest
i'm a fucking forest
when i swallow the forest
that i am
i am
green
when i swallow a bird
i see a round bird
& i swallow it
& it goes quiet inside me
when i'm a forest i am
looking out from the forest
& i am seeing
our love

all day wax is dripping into my mouth

all day i'm trying
to talk about
my candle wax stump of a head
all day my mouth is
a black yawn
filling with wax
all day i am saying
charlie brown words
as a sad bottom ·
what other ways are there to be dumb
one day i'm burned in the mouth
i think of getting away
like a squirrel might bleed
into shadows
the wax drips in

& people are like
what did you say
& i'm like
garaglk gara guh
& then
just the breathing is hard

bc i'm a reptile

someone said birds are reptiles
& i had to think
& then i thought goddamn
why so negative
& then this girl asked how's teaching
& i thought goddammit
one joke i like to say is that
i hate my students
that's a joke i guess
because it's true
& because people laugh
i'm afraid of getting cranky here at the bar
one of the guys here is a dad
he's inviting me to go trick-or-treating
what i want is a time machine
he says who doesn't
a couple of leaves together then
& that is when i start to feel stick

when the floor speaks it loves you

am i supposed to talk
about the drain
your feet or something
things i know
when you're half-dead you come to me
when the bottle has beat it out of you
or you're just too tired to stand
if not me to catch you
then something else
that's what keeps me here
not faith
or gravity
i'm too unlike you to be held
by the same stuff
but i know i'm good

even if i lose everything
there's this
moment of talking to you
you'll know
what a strange thing it is
to be loved
by something that is only a thing
& cannot love

i am a sociopath

am i very selfish
am i very unaware of others
i try but all i can see
are the windows all around you
that you send me in pictures
i know there is a woman close by
should i have said
what book i'm reading
that at least
may be something you can use
like a spoon or a fork
god help me
i do love you
i don't know if i do
but i do
if i would follow you into a cave

if i would put your foot in my mouth
if i would be naked all day
in front of you
i think i'm confusing you
with someone else

oh

yes
i would like to be
butter
room temperature
beat with an egg
& sugar
whipped into
stiff
peaks
on your chest
idk why
something that can melt
in your mouth
dissolve on your belly
& you can shit
out the same day

the complex human

i've been reading a lot
of sixteenth-century essayists
this girl today was like
sorry how i said u looked scared
which i'm sure she didn't
but there was
someone else
saying i was like a deer
i am thinking multiple things
feverishly
when the professor
looks at me in class

we need to fuck

i say something
& you say
we need to fuck
i think it's strange
what happens
part of you in me
i think it's ugly
even if i love you
your weird shape
it's important
that i am both
a woman
& not a woman
that i enter you the same
that i'm empty
& ashamed

that you both want it
& don't
the going under
the togetherness
that is sometimes less
sometimes more awful
than being alone

fold

i wasn't listening
i was thinking
fold you into me
remember that you used to fold
you'd get high & it would be
your favorite thing
my walls so invisible
so high
i can't get high
'cause who will take care of
the walls
i built so
carefully
you sneaky cocksucker
you are a fucking genius
to ever get around those walls

you're a goddamn expert
why don't i give you a day off
& let you just stand
somewhere
in a field
just look at you standing in a field
how your hair is
the skin that holds you
in a field
take pleasure in
your pleasure
in a field
or on a goddamn train in dallas
every present moment
i think DOOM
i think
like
death

i think i'm goddamn scared
of a field
& that you're standing
too far in it
& i've seen the earth catch
a black hole
& swallow
& i think i know death
& its empty fucking empty
& i think
i know
what's gonna happen
& that it's gonna be soon
so i think
if we could just
lie down
for a minute

everything is boring

i'd like to hide you
in my cunt
my cunt is a place
where you might sort out
your demons
everything is boring
i feel cavernous
i think beauty should be
worth
a lot more
i'd like to join a cult
where we fuck
& consort with
demons
but we can't afford it
poetry
can be so much

already
like fucking
when i pull you out of
my cunt
we are living together
in a crummy apartment

sex is weird

are you aware of my blood
it means
i have a permanent wound
lol
open wound
forever
i feel you
moving around inside my wound
it feels good
you are literally
inside my body
you fucking goon
no one will ever be good enough
to be inside my body
but here you are
inside the only body

i will ever have
i love you
lol
me & your cock are married now
me & your cock
are about to get a divorce
your cock
is about to throw up
inside the church

babies

your mood comes like a plague
thirty darknesses i cycle through
in one night
i think i'm caught
somewhere
in the math
when you calm
you cool
you coolly say
i don't want babies
as if babies raining down
from the ceiling
shook loose
stunned
by your appearance
in the hallway

thank u

yes
i am feeling very raw
like a wound rubbed for hours
or not very long
you say i'm sorry
it didn't last very long
& i spiral out
into the hole in your backboard
you just ripped open
without knowing it
it's no one's fault
i murmur
you say WHAT
for the sixteenth time today
& lean into me
in a way that is
terrible

i am spiraling
while you
are being someone
i imagined
you wouldn't believe
all the imaginary
thoughts
i'm having when i'm quiet
for instance
i just imagined your whole future
i imagined the word doom
i imagined a woman
spiraling alone
in a room
& it doesn't take much
imagining
then
to imagine
how little love can be

is it good

is it good i wanna say
to chain your heart to
another heart or
how do you do it
he says
i don't feel so good
that is what we say
for tonight
he says
what should i say
i say nothing
he says
i go to bed in
the land of no dreams
he mirrors me in his sleep
he begins to
undress me
this is a kind of

love
this sentiment
of needing to remove
my clothes in his sleep

it's ok

i like my body
but i like yours more
in the concavity of
your hipbone
just there
is where i die
i am born again
in your armpit hair
lost of course in
your crotch
okay if i love you
if i am insane
in love
caught in the spell
of your living body
it's alright

fuck

i deserve to be dead
i've worked
so
hard
& i'm pretty
like a
dead horse
pray over my stupid
wild
animal
body
take me
to the kitchen
with a cleaver
& your cock
i have pain in my heart

spring

it's still spring but
it feels like summer
i'm chewing
a pork chop
with my pants
hiked up the leg
& my sleeves rolled up
reading your poems
thinking about
fucking you
on the sofa
come to my sofa
i want to call you
bad names
so you can know
that i mean it

prying the damn sun out the damn sky

like crime
it's definitely going to happen
each pours out
their feelings
on the same day
if i could stop
loving you
if i could
begin
if i could lie
on the black street
for a minute
it swallows the flood
it's literally the day
the sun comes out

dutchman's pipe

how beautiful it was
to drown together in that
sweet milk
bath
your concrete floors
soft & hard
the dutchman's pipe
at the audubon house
a kind of robe i did wear
for a day or two
you think i forget everything
but i am past forgetting
i am in a new day now
of dead trees
where my hair is one
& what it says about you

chrysanthemums

i want to tell you it's okay
but the flowers have
one hundred eyes
& someone has left
the back gate open
when i say white
the flowers perk up
they are white
it's a bit of a shame
you start to say like
one day
i will explain
but you won't explain
what you will do is
continue to be a weed
the kind that separates

& rolls away
someone has forgotten
to give them a mouth

celebrity deathmask

i love you but
you are kind of dead to me now
i mean you refuse
to let me
suffocate you
with my hair
i keep it unwashed for you
literally bathe in camellias for you
not soap
the whole flower
not just the petals
then i have sex for you
on top of the petals
& then i flunk out of grad school

flowers

not sure what it was
that made me want to
pull up every
flower
out of the ground
or bush
&
you know
like
cover
myself
with the flowers
no one
was looking
i felt pretty
i guess

it's important
maybe
to feel that way
like
even
when no one is
looking
or
especially then
these are simple feelings

how long have i carried you

for these moments
even
with all my art
you answer me
with a word
i've gone ahead
into the stony river
it is greater than sex
i own it
& the trees
& the animals
that will hear me
when i have
mastered you
when i have
mastered myself

ooh

your silence is stunning
look at it
miraculous
the greatest thing you've ever done
& more frozen
so frozen it's like
past frozen
into
a white frozen sea
of cold ass motherfucker
what's nice about it
is
it's something i can walk across
look
i'm smashing it behind me
like a crazy river

i don't need your rearview
i need your silence
like
ooh
your vast fucking empty
so good to me
your sadness
so beautiful

this is why you must love me forever

what has happened to us
i'm afraid there is
something evil
inside
i'm afraid of—
a letter
a letter to everyone
an open-ended letter
please respond soon
i'm writing in the dark
i can't see
what i've written

i miss the world

he says there's something like a fire
& a fire comes
& i'm crying in a fire
he says ashes
& the fire is done
& i'm making a river
out of the ash
i'm making a beautiful river
& he's like
yes
he says
the sun is coming
& we are kids in a yard
& then
i can't understand the words

clash at demonhead

his mother holds me deeply
in a parking lot
a safety phrase
i'm battling demons
i've become
such
a total
bitch
parts of the narrative are missing
he digs
like a monk
he says because you're here
he taps my forehead with a pencil
he says you're not
paying
attention

where do you find the words he says
in the morning
in the fireplace
in my mother's breastbone
you learn to make them up

then the black train comes

then the black train comes
to spoil everything
then you say something
completely senseless
then the wall opens up
like an eye
& the train comes barreling through
clanging against the tracks
& the tall weeds bob & sway
& o gracious black
o great oblivion
i don't know why you care
about anything
other than me
but you do
& you say i have to sleep

& you say i can't see you
you need to make friends
o sweet
o sweet my love
i am the only friend you'll ever need

the most beautiful thing

the most beautiful thing
is a thing you made
i lay down beside its flatness
& swallow it
deep
deep
deep in the deep
arms unfurled
like a long white cloth
i bellow inside
with its
movement
i'm soft
in the underground
where the sky bows under me
like a bell

i wore a black dress on a green hill

& when the dark
cloud came
to look over
the lakes & the lavender
i was afraid
& tripped over
a dead root
& smacked my head on a stone

burn it in the yard

it would be better
if you were dead
or you could learn
to act like it
i collect your ephemera
& burn it in the yard
like a dead goose
everything past green
in the kitchen
the greatest thing of you
the fridge itself
compounded
in a toxic smoke
do you even
have any idea
it is not even nearly enough

put it in the bag motherfucker
i can't burn you
i can't even come close

sea wave

i'm laying right next to you
you are asleep
how does it feel to be your woman
again
i let go of myself
like the sea in the middle of a wave
so long so long

sleep

sleep until i forget you
until orange is blue

things that make my heart race

- cutting a long rope
- dreams of dead friends
- my phone ringing

happy birthday

you say
you're older now
my mother
sends a package
in the mail
i've been looking
at dreams
in them
i find
a new drug
organic
it's very hard
to operate
anyway
it isn't real

fat blue fish

you say did you say something
& the optimism in it
makes me feel like
there's something i could say
that could be the right thing to say
& the fat blue fish
fixed on the porcelain tub
that are meant to grip my feet
the two dimensional blue fish
that seem trapped
seem gulping for air
i know they can't mean anything

clouds

the next day
you came
& took each thing away
in a little procession
the doorknob
with the jasmine petal
on one end
the little yellow lighter
that had become
a part of my last solace
sitting in the doorsill
smoking too much
watching the clouds
hang
like ufos

a reason to be sad

well you finally got
a reason to be sad
you say
flowers ain't it
i guess i kind of
float
on a sea of rug
in a living room boat
i don't have
when you say
to stack some books
on your chest
& i feel the weight there
& it's kind of sad
& you say
how many people

got born today
it's 272,725 which is
a nice enough number
but it just makes me
feel worse

hammer time

i found a mound of dust
i'm breathing in all the years
i'm breathing the dead & dust
i'm literally made of poems now
i'm carrying my hammer
& hammering the floor
i'm hammering the air conditioning unit
hammer time
hammering my
loving you
i toss a hammer into the air
& catch it
& plow it
into a stump
i hammer the dust
i hammer the blanket of dust

i hammer the dust
i blanket the dust
i hammer you
i follow you into the mountain
hammer style
i hammer the mountain
i hammer the bird
i hammer the other bird
the other bird
is a bird
made of dust
i inhale the bird dust
i hammer the lung
i love the air
that the bird lives in
i hammer the sky

i'm in love with a wall

this is the second wall
i've been in love with
i'm happy to feel
like doing collage work again
it's very hard
& very brave
if you've ever left everything
& nobody will commend you
for the fact

i'm the only one who feels

some big thunder
is stomping through the river
& i am listening
nobody else is listening the way i do
i drop you out of this house
drop you out the floor like a cartoon
i can be the man now
& the woman
i can be the enemy
to whom you say
don't you know proper how to feel
i write all day
& i say everything
i listen to the sky
& i say everything
& nobody says much
i move real slow

clutch

we drove to a space
a long clearing
near the woods
where the towers
could be seen
busily all reaching up
in white glory
across in gloom
ready
that was all
traffic slowed
mightily
in the wake
for a moment
all together
held
for a moment
so ready to be crushed

the woods

how come you never took me
to the woods
there's nothing sad about
fucking under a tree or
watching a campfire go
but one thing is
i won't ever forgive you
for leaving me in the city
i never saw a river & the spiral jetty
i never saw a pink lake
with embers
or a goddamn snake
& whether or not that's true
is not my fucking problem
i can make a fire go
i can refrain from injury

i can pack light
& kick the dirt
but fuck it
i won't ever enjoy the woods

dream warrior

when i'm alone
in the woods
i need you
sometimes
& you are there
i can barely write this
he says when you dream
you aren't
alone
in your dreaming
i am there
i can barely move
when you sleep
with the windows nailed shut
in your crummy apartment
in the city

the six insects make it feel
close
what is far away
he says
i'm there
keep fighting
& if you want to
meet me for coffee

chopping wood poem

this is the poem i don't write
i just tell it to you
& watch it disappear
into your face
like everything
it's the story of chopping wood
which you will recall
part of the magic
is that you can give it away
to whoever you want

alone by you

& i hate
your flowers
you have learned
to be sweet &
your flowers
it is the time when
you know
it is the last time
you will see
the woman
& she is
the most beautiful
this time

acknowledgements

"sea wave" originally appeared in *keep this bag away from children* • "bc i'm a reptile" first appeared in *Sink Review* • the title "clash at demonhead" is taken from the movie *Scott Pilgrim vs. the World* • "i am the only one who feels" appeared in *The Nervous Breakdown* • "clutch" appeared in *Real Poetik* • "i wore a black dress on a green hill" appeared in *(wo)manorial* • "the woods," "i am a sociopath," "fold," "celebrity deathmask," "chrysanthemums," & "spring" first appeared in *Tenderloin* • "when i'm a forest," "confused what kind of animal i am," & "i am magic" first appeared in *Witch Craft Magazine*

Laura Theobald is a poet and author currently living in New Orleans. She recently earned her MFA in poetry in Baton Rouge. Her chapbooks include *edna poems*, *The Best Thing Ever*, and *eraser poems*. Her website is lauratheobald.net. She tweets @lidleida.

Printed by Imprimerie Gauvin
Gatineau, Québec